THE SECRET DOOR

CYNTHIA ROSS

"Too many devils, a lot of pain, and pretty smart from a B Girl."
DEBBIE HARRY

"A deeply moving, deeply felt collection of poetry—a raw, tender, poignant exploration of art, loss, change, and the one force that propels it all forward: love." It'll take you by the hand and grab you by the throat—sometimes both at once. You will gladly surrender to its beauty."
CLÉMENCE MICHALLON
Author, The Quiet Tenant

"Cynthia's poetry awakens hearts, seducing every detail and secret of life. She is a magnetic attractor for all of us who imagine love."
JULIANA VANNUCCHI
Fanzine Brazil

"Cynthia writes highly evocative words/ lyrics that can infiltrate the consciousness through an attractively self-effacing mode of presentation, enunciated with beauty and precision in real life performances. Perhaps it's because she doesn't consider herself a 'singer', that her voice is so cool."
PETER PERRETT

"Cynthia Ross writes from the deepest part of a wounded heart, locked in relentless combat with sadness and loss, always stepping away from the ledge and moving toward the joy that still exists out there, dazzling as an Eldorado enveloped in flames at midnight on Avenue A."
MAX BLAGG

Copyright © 2025 Cynthia Ross

Published Exclusively and Globally by Far West Press

All rights reserved. No part of this book may be reproduced in any form or by any electronic or mechanical means, including information storage and retrieval systems, without written permission from the publisher or author, except in the case of a reviewer, who may quote brief passages in a review. Scanning, uploading, and electronic distribution of this book or the facilitation of such without the permission of the publisher is prohibited. Your support of the author's rights is appreciated.

This is a work of fiction. All names, characters, businesses, places, events, and incidents are either the products of the author's imagination or used in a fictitious manner. Any resemblance to actual persons, living or dead, or actual events is purely coincidental.

www.farwestpress.com

First Edition

ISBN 979-8-9913506-1-7

Printed in the United States of America

Cover photo by Dave U. Hall
All inside photos by Cynthia Ross
All paintings Ian Wilson

For

Amanda Rogers
Dylan Rogers
Robin Schloss
Jackson Mintz
Lucasta Ross
Sole Zalba
Antonio Reyes
Michael D'Addario
Eva Chambers
Sam Hariss
Juliana Vannucchi
Jesse Malin

CONTENTS

ADIEU	9
I GO TO OTHER PLACES	10
DAMAGED	13
MYSTERY	15
REFRAIN	16
PAIN	17
EYES ON THE CEILING	18
WALKING DOWN 10TH STREET	20
ANGLES	21
STREETS	23
FEAR	24
FOR EVERMORE	25
GRIEF WALKING	27
STONES	28
DEATH DAYS	29
SAFE	30
BOXES	31
WHISPER	32
THREE	33
POSTCARDS	35
BED	37
EMPTY	38
SYMPHONY	39
READING	42
TIME	43
DEATH MARCH	44
WINGED WARRIORS	45
PRAYER	47
FALL	48
SEPTEMBER	49
BIRDS	50
DARKNESS	51
THE DANCE	52
DANCE INTO THE LIGHT	53
REFLECTION	54
INTROSPECTION	56

DREAMS AGAIN	57
THE VEIL	58
DEADICATION	59
HERE	60
HERE AND THEN GONE	61
BODY OF KNOWLEDGE	62
FLIGHT	63
GRACE	64
PAINT IT BLACK	65
DREAM	66
PATTERNS	67
MORNING	69
RESOLUTION	70
DAWN	71
TIME PASSES	72
INJUSTICE	73
MOURNING THOUGHTS	75
LOST	76
RITUAL	77
LOVE DIVINE	78
WILLING	79
UNSAID	80
LIKE LOVE	81
CHAIN	82
TEARS	83
DRIFTING	84
THERE IS	85
LOVE BECOMES YOU	87
A ROSE	89
EVA SAYS	90
THE TOWER	92
FADED	95
LOVE POEM 7	96
NOT LOVE	97
LONELY HEART OF SAINT VALENTINE	98
WITH LOVE	99
ILLUSION	101

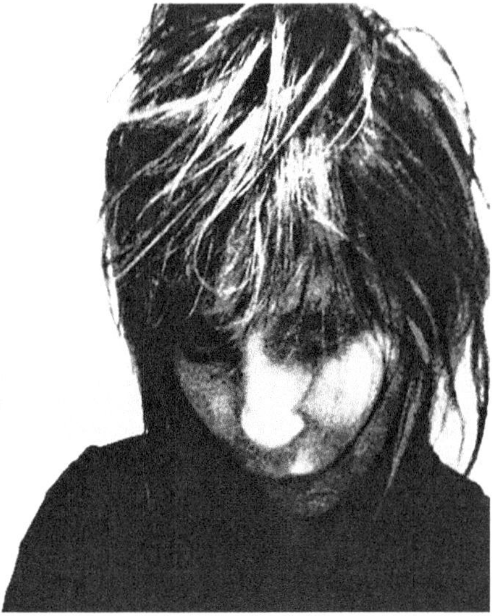

ADIEU

Today I say goodbye
dead lover, younger self
My habit of walking in the past
is making me unwell

Take down the heavy velvet curtain
It covers the stained glass
And hides the daylight
It muffles the sound of children singing

Lay it down with gilded memories
and love
Part of an old plan to protect myself
from pain

But now the pain
has overgrown within
And taken my name

Amidst clinging vines and
branches
I count the hours
Until night and darker darkness
to see if I'm still here

That heavy, velvet drape
Shields me from everything
Beauty, love and joy

Beside me st this moment
Inside if I breathe

I GO TO OTHER PLACES

I save towels, shirts and rags
that smell like my grandmother, my children,
my lovers, my friends.

My memories are colour, smell, emotion, sound.
Loud, strong, pungent, bright.

I go to other places when fear takes over

Open my heart and lungs, close my eyes and ears, lose control,
unknow all that I know about reality.
The outline of my body disappears.

I go to other places

I seem like I'm here ... Here in hell.
I smell and see that sad, lonely girl sitting in the corner crying,
hiding, ... waiting for a love that is never coming back.

I go to other places

I seek friends that feel like dead lovers.
Cold and pretty as the night.
I scour songs for melody and sadness,
words that mean something. Nothing works.

I reject happy. Melody bores me.
I don't count beats and bars.
Music is madness.
Math is lines and patterns.

Of course I don't count.
I've never counted.
I was terrible at math and
never meant much to anyone.

I don't count

I look for lovers that feel like dead friends.
Hot and ugly as the night.
They don't count either.

I throw away garbage as soon as I get it.
It clings to me.
I attract it, like I deserve it.

The smell, the colours, pungent and potent, heavy, mixed up.
Garbage is never orderly.
I like order. I don't like math.

Trash. Garbage. Men who rot. Not garbage men, just men who are garbage.
Garbage men attract me. I want a man who would throw me out like that.
Pick me up like that ... Hold me for a minute then crush me.
They know how to do their job.

I don't like lawyers, doctors, bankers, men with money.
Men without money. Men with opinions based on facts
they learned in school. Men who are good at math.
Musicians who count.

I like crazy men, guys with problems, boys with bad attitudes,
strong in their imperfection. Pretty repels me. Chipped teeth, scars
visible and invisible ... The ones who won't let me run them.
I want those damaged souls to mesh with mine.
I don't like men. I don't like myself or math either.

I don't count

It's three am. I can't sleep.
Why am I writing about garbage, lovers, sad girls crying on corners,
men, math, boys, rags, and rotten friends.
Sadness, old smells, scars, imperfection?

I must want sex.
Maybe I should clean the house.

DAMAGED

Told you I am damaged
And the reasons why
Told you I am damaged
Baby it's no lie

The death camps and the heroin
The men, they all died
The children that I gave away
The ones I kept behind

I told you I am damaged
And baby it's the truth
No one can make me whole again
Not even love nor you

There is no magic surgery
No needle or no pill
Time it will not heal me
It's not that kind of thing

I hung out at the Factory
With all the Superstars
They will not take me back now
They shut it down with bars

I walk the streets of New York City
You can't see my pain
Buried in the rubble
Nothing is the same

A jewel glimmers in the sun
Silver on the ground
A single shiny safety pin
That symbolized our sound

Now it lies forsaken
A medal from the war
The one that we were waging

Not the one before

So simple in its beauty
So sad in its decline
I still see the beauty
It pierces through my mind

My mind is filled with madness
My heart it's filled with you
I stitched up all the sadness
But somehow it seeps through

Counting on my fingers now
To take me to the truth
And memories of ecstasy
I'm counting on that too

Memories are fading
Tears run dripping dry
I told you I am damaged
And the reasons why

We met out on the battlefield
The streets so bright and tough
Time just walked right by me
They said I'd had enough

MYSTERY

Yeah baby it's a mystery
The things you do to yourself
Night time it's a mystery
You're all by yourself

You cry tears
You call out
Words sound strange
Get paid, your future's made
But your life it goes on and on

Downtown's got no bright light shining
Lonely on the street
Downtown's got no nightlife living
No, not on the street

I watch as you slip away
A little every day
That man downtown keeps calling you
And you decide to stay

Downtown's got no bright lights shining
It's lonely on the street
Downtowns got no nightlife living
No, no not on the street

I know you're no ones miracle
I've seen how much you pay
Living daily misery
What can I do to make it be okay?

So alone among the crowd
Still looking for more
So alone among the crowd
Still looking for, still trying to find more

REFRAIN

The mystic said
Cast out past pain
Pain is like traffic
It comes again

Don't soak in sorrow
The sayer said
Costs if you borrow
Burrows in bed

Memories fade
ODs don't blame
The vampire's still stalking
For more of the same

Out in the streets
All in the game
The actors have changed
But not the refrain

PAIN

Know you well

In the dark.

Feel your comfort

Wrapped around.

Hands, belts, words, fire -

Do not touch me.

You sit inside my human form.

A vulture waiting for weakness.

A disease wanting to kill me.

My fear and sad self loathing.

My heart beating its death march.

My anger never seen.

You are with me to the end.

I am hiding. I am ugly.

I am melting.

I can leave at any time.

I have ways to fly while walking.

When feelings touch me, I go.

No one knows.

EYES ON THE CEILING

We faced another winter
Waking up wanting
Shaking and needing
Aching not feeling
Begging and pleading
Eyes on the ceiling
Legs that kept thrashing
And shallow deep breathing
Then there was stopping
The weakness of talking
And facing reflection
Self judgement, rejection
Memories fading
Still you stood stalking
Resolve began waning
And heartbreak's cold calling
The harsh light of morning
Eyes on the ceiling
Aching not feeling
Hid in the cupboard
And waited a year
Re-entered with fear
Asserted control
With feelings and sadness
Time, it just passes
Eyes on the ceiling
Begging and pleading
Aching not feeling
Shaking and needing

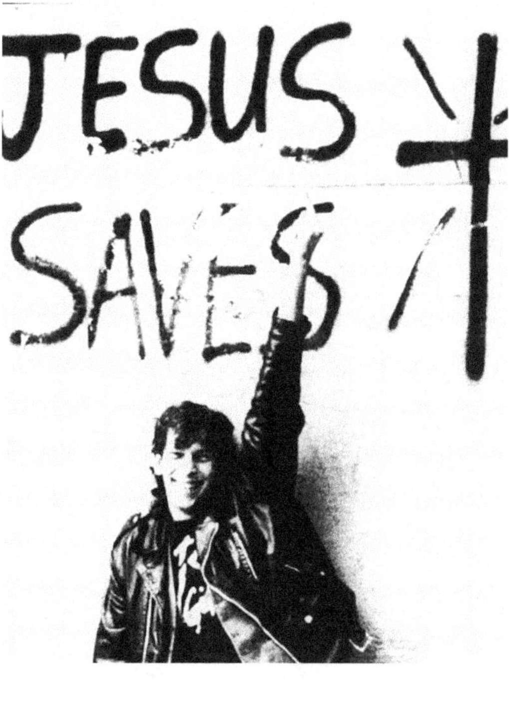
JESUS
SAVES

WALKING DOWN 10TH STREET

Songs drifting from windows
And stories told on stoops have disappeared

Births and deaths are nobody's business
No longer shared with neighbours or supers or stoop kids

Now
Only the buildings remember

Nothing is different
Everything has changed

We ate oatmeal for every meal
And dried dishes on boards over bathtubs in kitchens

It was 1982 and time moved slow
Billy rolled pennies for cigarettes and milk

Morning walks meant something else entirely

On 10th Street there was no anxiety
Because most days we were too high or too dopesick to feel anything

Walking down 10th Street

Now
Only the buildings remember

ANGLES

Like terrestrial twins
We split into a thousand little pieces of dna
When love left
We scattered like mice
On floorboards with cracks
And knots and remnants
Of crumbs
Our only direction angles
Angles to avoid
Angles to adhere
Angles to escape
Angles not circles
Angles not lines
Angles not squares
Disconnected and scattered
Like mice
On cracked floorboards
Squeezing through holes
Scanning for crumbs
Pittering and pattering
Out of time

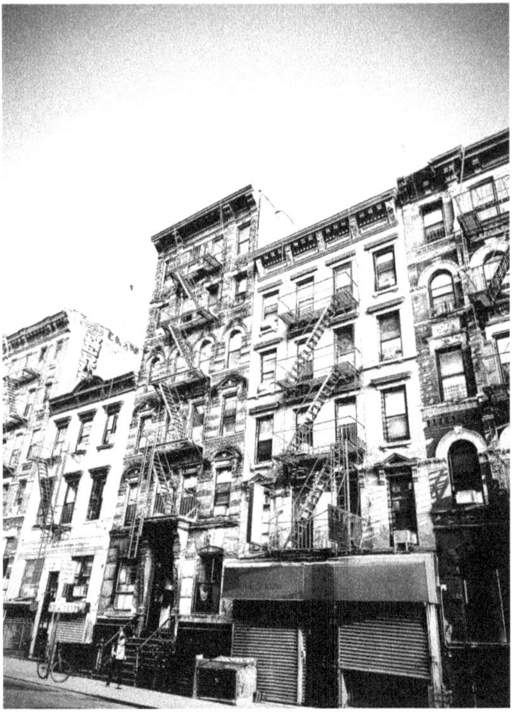

STREETS

The streets are museums

They hold history and artifacts

Images, smells and sounds

Listen closely beneath the din

You'll come upon the shadow of the past

And in the shadow of the past

Amidst the ancient ruins

Amidst destruction and desecration

Sighs and wistful whispers

Tales of bygone days

Sacred stories seep

Through crevices and cracks

That even endless concrete cannot seal

FEAR

My fear
Hides in boots, books
That jacket at the back of my closet
In pockets, cups, bowls
Drawers, memories
Anything with space

Breathe out
Comes back
Age old culprit
Rides on thought
Thrives on time
Killer of joy
Love denier
Sleep depriver
Executioner of ease

Moves like a mugger
Follows footsteps
Runs down stairs
No escape
Stands on corners
Jumps over buildings
Prey, pray

My fear
Does not wear black
Sounds like sirens
Only louder
Walks through walls
Changes its face

Hangs in doorways
Street corners, hallways
Sidewalk crawler
Bedside companion
Night time screamer
Graveyard digger

When death comes knocking
Hope fear steps away

FOR EVERMORE

And when the velvet mornings
'Light
Upon your skin so softly

In the dawn

I cry
I cry
I cry

Knowing how the daylight wanes
The tides
Recede
In your veins

Your eyes

They cry
They cry
They cry

On teardrops we are cast adrift
Sails set off for minor lift
And memories, they float on by
On mirrors shining in the sky

We cry
We cry
We cry

Your beauty is a fleeting gift
An image for the evermore
Captured in the sacred heart
Tethered to a secret door

As time defies our wanting wish
And takes your body from the room
I cling to what I know I'll miss

For evermore your love will loom

In morning sun and evening light
On mirrors shining in the sky
As time defies our wanting wish

We cry
We cry
We cry

And when this velvet morning
Breaks upon your silken skin
So softly

In the dawn

I cry

GRIEF WALKING

I am grief walking

Wrapped in shrouds of longing

Longing for you in form

I shed the guise of belonging

Feeling forlorn

I stutter step to mourn

As I step

Over sidewalk cracks

Remembering times

Love kept us warm

Morning brings another storm

Of fresh tears

On cold concrete

Soles worn, souls warn

And inform the loss of form

I am grief walking

In the low light of morn

STONES

Names on stones
In fields of grass
Filled with remains
Yet nothing remains

And carving names
To mark the graves
That name the past
Won't make life last

But stone is strong
And memories long
And names are given
When form is born

When it ends
We carve in stone
And stand on dirt
To send love home

DEATH DAYS

I wear death wrapped around me like armour

Closely connected to lost love and past life

Sadness from the first breath

Despair with the first step

Now I have lost the safety of separation from self

And don't know who I am

I've shed the serpent skin

And sad sad sins

And when I awake

I see the light of last days

Rising suns roll like an abacus

Counting last breaths

And memories reflect love

Not loss

And sunrise is so bright

That I am lost

SAFE

My memory of feeling safe
Is locked away in your arms
Held tight with ropes and talismans
Bound by younger selves

I inhale old photos like a last breath filled with longing
And question why you left
To walk through vacant lots
And abandoned thoughts

With feelings bereft of time and place
Your jacket no longer shields me
From weather, loneliness, danger
Bad music or myself

I look through boxes
To find the sacred armour we shared
Like food, shelter, lust
And memories of feeling safe

Because my memory of feeling safe
Is locked away in your arms

BOXES

Shuffle through boxes
Memories remind me who I am
Searching soul
Quiet girl
Sad sister
Good student
Ballet dancer
Music lover
Avid reader
Aspiring artist
True love

Travel through time
Images flood my mind
First step
Girl band
Young love
Motherhood
Sky scrape
City block
Bass player
Lone survivor
Still hope

WHISPER

I stand in the shadows
Head in the clouds
Hide dreams
In ripped pockets of old coats
Hung in my closet
Beautiful shrouds

Do not deny me
Says some whisper
Do not betray me
Screams dead lover
Do not avoid me
Says my own voice

I search through my past
For signs I exist
Crumpled photos frayed and torn
Tell stories
Shoes recount journeys
Lingerie stirs longing

Do not betray me
Says some secret
Do not deny me
Says my story
Do not speak
Says my own voice

THREE

Gaze into the cupboard
Dishes stacked
I don't need four
Four is for families
And couples with friends

I use
One bowl
One cup
One glass

I only needed one death
You gave me
Three
One for each love

Three bands
Three men
Three children

Dish cracked
Now three

My full cupboard
Expresses loneliness

I spot a baby spoon
Four now it says
Three plus one
Besides, you forgot yourself
When you counted

Stop looking at dishes
Close the cupboard
Open the door
Three steps

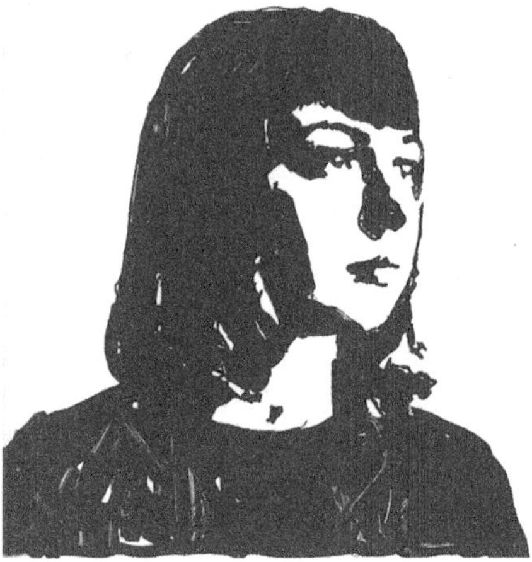

POSTCARDS

We shared everything
Cut and coloured each other's hair
Sought out cheap rags
Men's coats
Tight pants
Old women's shoes
Blurred gender
Threw together looks
Wore black
Rebelled against rules
Made music
Ran clubs
Meshed art, film, literature

There were no stylists
Or makeup artists for bands
We emulated and riffed off icons of cool
Smoking hot like Brando, Dean and Elvis
Wild and tasteful like Hepburn, Liz and Bridget
Mysterious like Anita, Nico, and Marianne
Good Bad like the Shangri-Las
Soulful like Laura, Ronnie, Dylan, Keith
Sad like Leonard and Lou

Children of the Beat Generation
We read books and poetry
Watched old movies
Listened to jazz, blues, pop and country records
Danced, talked and touched

We went on a perpetual journey
Some left
Lost on highways
And other accidents of time and place

For those of you still travelling
Please send postcards

BED

The bed is empty beside me
Filled with memories
And stories

It pushes me to the edge
My side that was your side
When you were here

Now I curl tightly
Holding on to nothing
But feelings

The empty side is full
The full side
Is empty

EMPTY

The cup is empty and fragile
Fine china, etched with flowers
Dripping with ancient beauty
Gilded images from another time

And in its emptiness and fragility
The cup shared stories
Saw families come and go
Lived in several countries

Knew lovers, desire, ambition, loss
Started as part of a set
The cup is empty and fragile
Sometimes full and warm

Fine lines on its surface

Ageing but not broken

SYMPHONY

I'm tired of the death march
It drives me to a fugue state
I reach for a memory
To escape the dismal drone

Lines longer
Spaces shorter
Notes percolate
I can hear the coffee pot
On grandmother's stove

A symphony

Slow and soft
Then speeding up
Staccato
Crescendo
Steady and strong
Notes low and even
Steam rising like a cloud

The aroma
Dark, rich, warm
Fills the room
Fills the house
Wafts through windows
Sound, taste, smell, rhythm
Feels like home

A symphony

In the kitchen

Lessons learned
Lessons taught
Look into each other's eyes
Listen
Notice
See

Each placemat a snapshot
Each chair a seat
A felt sense of belonging
A place a place a place
Seen heard felt
I remember that

Meals delicious
True or not
Stories meaningful
Discussions deep
Or superficial

We sit in presence
Touch, taste, smell
I remember that
Perspective of a child

In the kitchen

Sermons
Rituals
The intersection of god and man
Orderly and dreamlike
Expansive and practical
A relational meeting place

Lessons and recipes
Trials and errors
Plans and dreams
Taste, touch, sound

I forget the death march
Lost in the symphony
Coffee calls out louder
Taste, touch, smell

Dancing in the kitchen
With my younger self
Teaches me the steps
I used to teach to her

Spinning, floating, free

I inhale repeatedly
Inhale inhale inhale
Dance to the symphony
Drift along on memory

Spinning, floating, free

READING

Reading offers a door of perception, integration or separation
Emotional thunderstorms and feeling clouds occupy thoughts
Ingested, dissected, rejected, digested, accepted
Questions enter closed quarters to stir stews of stagnant rhetoric
If life was an open book
Words would be clearer, neater, happier
Like nursery rhymes or fables
Instead of mysteries and horror stories scattered in dust

TIME

I am giving up my battle with Time
She announces like a headline

Then covers the mirror
Lowers her eyes to avoid reflection

Steps out of her body to deny desire
Stays indoors to suspend seasons

Wears black
Hide scars under makeup

Locks doors
Turns away to escape feeling

Seals the box of memories
Dismisses sadness on death days

Does not listen to music
Walks in crowds to disappear

Time looks away for a second
Then finds her through Fear

DEATH MARCH

We have gone silent

Our ears deafened by the sound

Of dead ancestors wailing

Bodies paralyzed by feeling

As every past pogrom of previous generations

And generations before

Echoes

Taken back to the train cars and and tents and deserts of denial

And the death march to the camps

We are not sleeping

We are walking awake to our death

Our bodies tense

In knowing the outcome

Always alone

Always facing death

There is something to be said for the familiar

A certain comfort an oracle denotes

Another dance with death

Another march for land

WINGED WARRIORS

When part of you dies
With people and time
Something survives
Darkness and light
Day and night

Morning denies comfort
Time marches on
Like foreign soldiers
Singing sad songs not sad enough
In perfect time

The streets have changed
Melodies burn my brain
All minor keys and discord
Sung by
Angels who are not angels
But winged warriors
Carrying messages

Winds that cannot breathe
Memories etched in pain
Sad songs without refrain
Whispered stories without endings
In ancient language without words

There is no safety or salvation or sunlight

Hummers hum
Love dies again
Over and over
Repeating lines
When part of you dies
With people and time

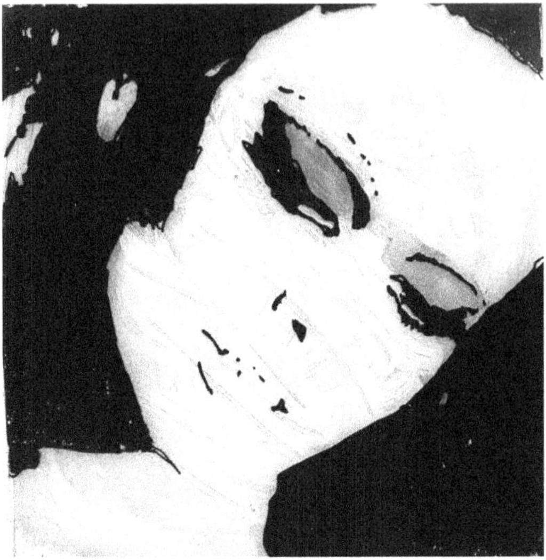

PRAYER - Ode to Leonard Cohen

Your voice meanders through my mind in minor monotone hymns
Solemnly swearing
Permanently praying
Forever melancholy
Soothing and familiar in its sadness

The open wooden drawer you hid your opium in
Describes the feeling when love leaves
Makes me reach inside
For a promise
As empty as the drawer

You of fallen robins, tea and oranges
Diamonds in the mines
Birds on wires, funeral pyres
Diamonds in the mines

And when you say you don't think of her that often
You are lying
Not betraying
Your way to worship our Angel of Eternal Fire

Oh you of fallen robins, tea and oranges
Diamonds in mines,
Birds on wires, funeral pyres
Famous blue raincoats, lovers waiting to come back
Places by the river, flowers for hitler

We wait in darkness again
On streets that are museums
Beds mausoleums
Floors full of holes
Doors that don't close
In books with burns
And youth that yearns

To find your reflection

FALL

With fall comes fallen
Feelings soon frozen
By winter's gaze
Fallen not forgotten
Coloured by autumn
Buried in snow
Sprung by spring
Heated by summer

The cold and the heat
The fall and defeat
The sun and rebirth
Our short time on earth

Morning and night
Darkness and light
Love and despair
And fall in the air

SEPTEMBER

It's the first of September
And as with all Septembers past
We remember
Summer to fall
Octaves of October
Leaves in November
Drifts to December
As summer meets fall
September to all

BIRDS

These dreams that are not dreams
But memory
Appear when we are ready
They fly like little birds
Above our consciousness

Singing songs we cannot hear

Theses stories that are not stories
But truths
Held in our bodies
Our bodies that are not bodies
But vessels

These loves that are not loves
But attachment

Each little bird a messenger

Light permeates the darkness
As darkness veils the light
Vision and insight
Illuminate the secret corners

Mind body
Body mind
Time an illusion
Memory a connection

Each little bird a messenger

Dreams, memory, stories, insight
Time, vessels, truths, love, light
Every night s journey towards freedom

The bird sings to announce daylight

DARKNESS

When my pain met your pain
We knew it wouldn't work
Too damaged by betrayal
Too tortured by the world

My soul looked through your soul
And somehow saw the sun
So brilliant in the darkness
Caught me on the run

Couldn't look into your eyes
For fear I'd see myself
Dancing in the moonlight
My love was on a shelf

With treasured books and photographs
Memories and fears
Collecting dust, I felt no lust
Been that way for years

Gazed into the darkness
Walked right through your pain
Filled with longing, long time waiting
Now I dance again

THE DANCE

No longer frozen in time
With a nudge the second hand moves
It caresses the face
Gliding beautifully past gilded numbers
Like a dancer in the corps de ballet
Plié plié
Marking memories and touching feelings
Twirling incessantly
Around the face
A pirouette
In time
Forward movement
En pointe
A stirring of rhythmic sound
Heard as a heartbeat
Felt as a breath
Second hand leaping
Gracefully in time
Jete jete
Flight flight towards the sky
Chausse releve
Eleve
Second act
Battement tendu
Graceful curtsy
Arms tell stories
In time in time in time
Dance of the swans
The intensity jumps
The magnificence of Nureyev in the Bolshoi Ballet
Before he defected
The beauty of his performances at The Royal Ballet
with Dame Margot Fonteyn
19 years apart in age, always together
Two dancers, one soul in time
Moving like a clock, flying like freedom
Soaring like magic
Vision of a child witnessing greatness
Burned brightly in the mind's eye forever
The dancer and the dance

DANCE INTO THE LIGHT

May I make new mistakes
The old ones are my jailers

May I escape the prison of perfection
The judge is my reflection

May I shed the shackles of fear bound in my body
They no longer protect me

May I leap into love and self love
With abandon not trance

May I dance into the light
The half light is darkness
It no longer serves me

May I express hidden thoughts
And speak unspoken feelings
They are poetry

REFLECTION

She took off the shackles
She thought were locked

She walked through the door
She thought was locked

She walked on the stage
And threw out the lock

The clock tick talked
Said time was the lock

Thoughts circled round
In time with the clock

Fear stood in the crowd
Said don't speak out loud

Stay in your box
With clocks, thoughts, and locks

Then Sunshine spoke up
Saying you have a choice

Those thoughts in your head
Are nothing but noise

Today is new
Your thoughts come from you

Choose people and things
Who shine and are true

Who speak with love
Who see with love
Who wake with love each day

A reflection of you

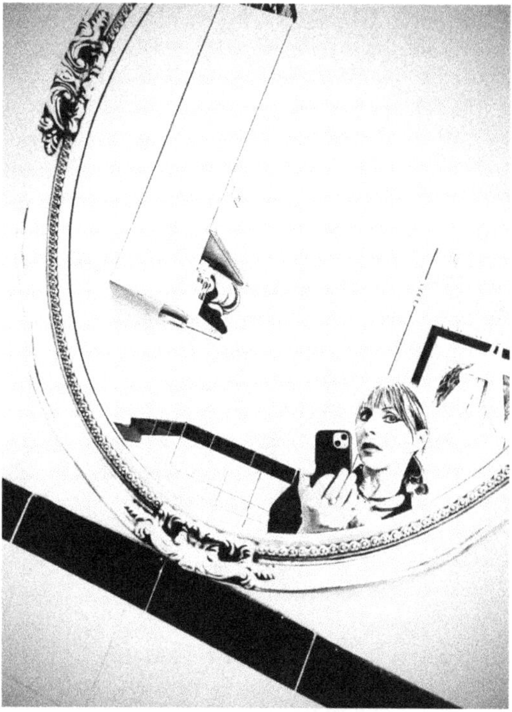

INTROSPECTION

Came when I wasn't ready
Made me wait
Stood tall upon insecurities
Overlooked strengths

Underestimated value
Because of you
I see who I am

DREAMS AGAIN

Memories emerge freely
And fill our dreams with names
Situations and events so vivid
That we are reliving, feeling, submerged in happiness and sadness nightly
When waking, there is a form of exhaustion from overstimulation
We are using some parts of our mind
For the first time since childhood
A new growth of thoughts, ideas
and
Possibilities emerge clearly from
The silence
Even the birds start singing
At 3 am and the songs sound new

THE VEIL

Made this journey often
Through ecstasy and pain
Doesn't scare me baby
I'd cross that street again

Lessons learned with longing
Loss and some betrayal
None of it is real
Behind the thin black veil

Used to gaze up to the clouds
And watch the world spin by
Thought I could be anything
And fly from town to town

Gravity is waning
Reality is loud
Getting harder daily
To stay down on the ground

Hide behind my thinking self
Lose myself in time
Used to be here baby
Now I float on by

DEADICATION

Try to sweep my mind
Of memories and time
And love assigned to plots
In graveyard buried spots

Hear it in my heart
Think it in my thoughts
It colours every day
You can't wipe love away

HERE

Fear surfaces with that third breath

As the mind lurches into future thoughts of mountains and lists

The heart reminds us that love is here in the moment

It is here

Surrounding us in presence

With sounds here to anchor us in presence

Beauty here before our eyes

Breathe again the fifth breath that releases fear to endless oceans

Where it travels with life's waves

And becomes small in the distance beyond distance

Drifting drifting drifting

Into endless space

HERE AND THEN GONE

Staying becomes harder
Good times seem farther
But what of those times
We hold in our minds

We block out the sun
Live life on the run
Long for the past
For futures we grasp

Stand in the shadows
Each day a battle
While presence is here
It's here beyond fear

Not in the mind
Or memory or time
Or things that we want
It's here and then gone

Notice the trees
The flowers, the leaves
The light in the morning
And dusk's sweet belonging

See through the eyes
The music that cries
The love in the heart
An expression of art

Not in the mind
Nor memory or time
Or things that we want
It's here and then gone

BODY OF KNOWLEDGE

In the floating up above
I escaped
But escaped love

Fear of entering
Kept me safe
From the facts
From the pain

From the facts
From the loss
I survived
But paid the costs

And my children
Paid the price
Of my distance
Fear and loss

Now I'm finding
My way in
To the body
To begin

In the floating
Up above
I survived
But escaped love

Not too late
Not too shamed
Not too silenced
To speak again

FLIGHT

Boots float like feathers
Above the ground which does not ground
Breaths of fear waft under and through to take flight
Amidst brief moments of happiness
That soar with sunshine
Clouds cloud
Trees shade and shelter
Birds take note and sing along
Flying above ground which holds its ground
Boots touch down
Earth sighs sounds
Dreams meander
Like water
Wishing and whooshing
Rising to the stars

GRACE

A breath, a space
A pause filled with grace
In letting go
Past is not erased

It quiets the din
Softens within
Makes room for presence
Light to come in

In holding the woes
History knows
The past takes control
No room for flow

A breath, a space
A pause filled with grace

PAINT IT BLACK

Decisions are the pushy part of life
Make you move when you would hold on tight
Paint it black
Swear it's white
Say it's day
But it's the night
Time to move
Still you fight

Decisions force feelings
Some not nice
Make you move
When you would hold on tight
Paint it black
Swear it's white
Resist too long
Lose all sight

Lose insight
Deny the light
Time is now
Fight or flight

DREAM

And when I wake
There is a Dream
A lot like life
A gift it seems
For every day
For every night
When I rise
There is a Dream
There is a Dream
So clear and real
A lot like life
A gift
A Dream

PATTERNS

I am in a hospital with an asylum, a detox and a section for people with snake and spider bites. We're all on lockdown and I need to escape. The walls are dingy hospital green. The beds are those iron army cots with striped ticking mattresses barely covered by flat white sheets worn and way past their prime. There are no curtains, just ugly brown metal school lockers between each bed. I remember noticing the beauty of the terrazzo floor and wishing they still made them.

It's quiet and loud at the same time. No one is talking, yet the place is filled with loud echoing sounds. Sounds normally not loud. Breathing, sheets brushing, hands and legs moving, throats swallowing, stomachs gurgling and the odd moan. I feel completely detached.

The nurses are like white robots. In and out they come in sequence gliding forwards, dispensing pills and liquids in white cups followed by Dixie cups filled with water. Then gliding backwards, face forward, through the many doorways. I begin to count the intervals between this dance of the cuckoo clock nurse brigade. One Mississippi, two Mississippi, three Mississippi, four Mississippi … How long between rounds? I time footsteps, doors opening and closing, meds, water, sleep and lighting.

I lie in that bed, sweat soaked from fever, hair sticking to my head and wearing a hospital gown with blue and white circles. I stare at the circles and notice they appear to grow larger and touch when the nurses come close and shrink to mere dots when they leave. It was as if everything was moving in some way. I needed to figure out the patterns. Then I can find the spaces.

I needed to check that I was here for a reason, not just a prisoner, so I looked down at my right knee below the calf. There are three large bites shaped like islands, red and swollen gouges in my skin, with a fourth smaller dot drifting in the sea. It's ugly. I feel sick and scared. I quickly cover them with one of those hospital issue blankets made to look like they were machine knit. More patterns.

I had to get out or I would never get well. That was my thought pattern over and over in my head. My chance would come in three seconds and I would have seven minutes to get out. I found some exotic hair product in the locker beside my bed. It turned my hair black and changed the texture so I could make it stand up. I quickly stole the clothes from the locker and put them on. They belonged to the girl next to me.

I hid in the basement where the detox was until the nurses went off shift. I followed them out getting lost in the crowd of what seemed like hundreds. I kept thinking about my hair and how much I liked it this way, especially the feel. I tried to picture the name on the container, but then I kept imagining that it was really that poisonous type of foam insulation because I had yellow goo on my hands. Finally I got through the gates and ran down the street.

I woke up suddenly like I was being chased. I have those chasing dreams often. I had not escaped. I was in that bed. I looked at my leg. The spider bites were real. They looked like islands gouged out of my skin, red, hot and swollen. I had a fever. Maybe they were going to amputate my leg in that hospital with an asylum, a detox and a section for people with snake and spider bites.

MORNING

When morning becomes the enemy
And sleep denies rest
Nightmares flail and flash
No longer dreamlike but lifelike
The endless regurgitating
Repetition of memories
Rewound, re wired
Replayed
Filled with pain and regret
Poor choices
Transgressions toward myself and others
The day does not welcome me
The streets do not direct me
The sunlight shines behind me
The rain falls on me

But then the words of Bob Dylan
A candle, coffee and an old lamp offer comfort
A slight shift in mindset
And the courage to open my notebook
Even if I write three words
And they are not what 'I am supposed to be' writing about
I am taking a step towards light and forgiveness

RESOLUTION

Out of the ashes
She rose to reclaim
The self that was waiting
To state her name

DAWN

Dark rooms full of strangers
Mark birthdays of dead friends
Cacaphonic emulators
Pretending to pretend

Suffocating circulating
Walking to the end
Hollow hallways filled with noise
Then mourning light ascends

Morning shines on new ideas
Silence brings new songs
Artists paint new paintings
It's life or death each dawn

TIME PASSES

Time passes like the first friend
The one who walks ahead in dreams
Or meanders behind in memories
Laughter echoes
Music vibrates
But time plods and plots
Races and lags
Time so fleeting
Deftly denies feeling
And runs out the door
As we wait for more

INJUSTICE

I walk alone
Sadness again
Tears don't stop
In knowing, in being, in feeling

You snap up the packaged story
Of the past I lived
Wear it like a costume

Lies prevail
Priced to fill select pockets
Dead men can't tell tales or truths

My ears drip with sad salty water
Youth a memory
Filled with love and fierce righteousness
Heart breaking heartbreaking

Loyalty is out of fashion
It's in the SALE bins
Headed for the trash
No value in today's economy

I don't care if you like me

Today I am true
You can't buy that in any shop
Or book or poem or fake band
In a city that no longer exists

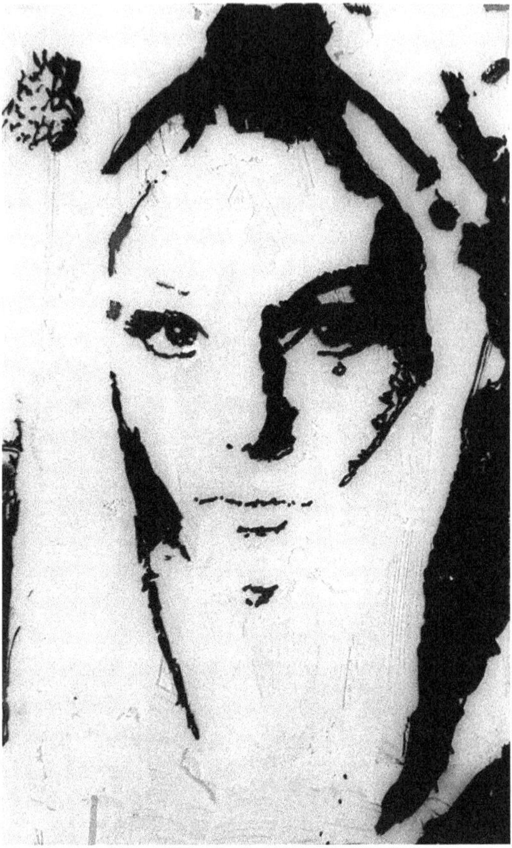

MOURNING THOUGHTS

We are not of this world
He whispers in sadness
The magic has left
Light is dark
They're killing our art
Dreamers gave notice
He weeps as he exits

We are not of this world
She calls out in glee
Look to the clouds
Run through the ruins
Listen to songs
Pour over pages
Old news is dead

The world that is gone
Left only in form
Do not cry forlorn
Each day new dreamers are born
To march through the storm
And bring out the treasures
That one day they'll mourn

LOST

In bygone days there was a quality called honour
It disappeared with truth
And flew beyond the clouds
The clouds that guard the sun
And rain upon the ruins
To wash away the dirt
That covers all the hurt
And glistens falling down
To search for what we've lost

And we are lost

RITUAL - for Anita

Photograph your cherry blossoms
Choose your rose tattoos
Me, I'll stick with black and white
Used to trust the news

Strummer strummed his protest songs
Johnny sang the blues
Brothers in arms
Scorned your charms
But wore your worn out shoes

The colour line was drawn with cash
Banks and prisons, schools
Institutions filled with bars
Privatised the news

Heaven waits and angels sing
A hymn, a prayer, a pew
High Priestess crossed from earthly realm
More than just a muse

The see ers see
The stoners stone
The singers sing
The prayers pray

The clingers cling
The moaners moan
Knowing she is coming home

Her beauty found it's rightful home
All are waiting at her throne
Knowing she is coming home

Her presence shines
And leaves a void
Time is time
We leave alone

LOVE DIVINE

Gather memories in a bowl
Life lived fully, heart and soul
What's the feeling each one calls
Smooth and soothing, sharp and fine
Stones and pebbles, suns and moons
Loves and losses, haunted ruins

In the counting count me in
In the space beneath the din
In the time, in the score
In the thoughts that block the door

Birth and death marked in time
In the thoughts, in the mines
In the space between the lines
In the heart shines love divine

Love and loss, heart and mind
Breathe the breaths and freely find
Find the space past the time
See the light of love divine

Walk and fly, live and die
Set out fresh, see the sky
Dance on clouds passing by
Feel the feel of love divine

WILLING

I will not write a will
Won't write down my wants
I cannot kick a can
Or have you haunt my haunts

I am different baby
Don't say what I see
I will not write a will
Or breathe away the breeze

I dance alone in darkness
Dream in daylight sun
I wake up when the sun sets
Move so fast, I run

You stand there in the shadows
I dare you to come out
I will not write a will
A deed to death is dumb

I read it in the paper
The headline said it best
She did not write a will
And will not ever rest

She dances in the moonlight
We see her pale blue skin
She did not write a will
So nothing left behind

I leave your world with questions
And answers I deny
I will not write a will
My will to live just died

UNSAID

All the words I did not say
And the prayers I did not pray
All the love I keep at bay
And the notes I wait to play

All the breaths I have to take
And mistakes I've still to make
All the songs I've yet to sing
And the family in the wings

All the friendships yet to form
And the love behind the storm
All the stories still untold
And the gift of growing old

All the stories still untold
And the gift of growing old
All the words I wait to say
Keep me here another day

LIKE LOVE

Memories flood back and surround me,
A hug that becomes a chokehold
Squeezing so tight that breath is not possible,
Yet tears flow at will

Let go I demand,
But secretly cannot allow it

When those memories go,
I'll float like dust into the ether
The outline of my body will disappear
Form will cease to exist

Tears flow

Like love

CHAIN

Prison of my mind
Keeping me confined
Swimming in the pain
Kinda like the chain

Keep me tied and bound
Hold me to the ground
Take me to the place
Feelings get erased

TEARS

Tears
Glisten like
Small shimmering seas
Reflections that wave
Toward the horizon

They flow with wind
Winding, whooshing
Dripping, dropping
In waves rolling
Toward the shore

Love floats on waves
Endless horizon
Endless distance
Endless time

Life focuses and forecasts
Pushing with purpose
Bobbing and sailing
Toward the shore

Life walks with wants
Trudging down paths
Of present and pasts
Searching for insight

The heart drifts out to sea in a salty tear

DRIFTING

I long to read to you by candle light
And hold you gently
like a child

Kiss your eyelids
Smell your hair

As your head rests safely in the
Hollow of my shoulder
I want to touch
Your cheek
Lightly stroke the sacred inner
fold
of your elbow

Trace the winding blue rivers of
your veins
softly
as they swerve in and out of
uncharted territories
then whoosh through channels
under covers

I want to taste
Your finger
and your thumb

I want
To inhale your exhale
In perfect and imperfect time
With your heartbeat

And savour that
Small
Final
Sigh

As you drift off to sleep
And I drift awake to desire

THERE IS

I AM nervous about REAL LIFE
About expressing FEELINGS
In REAL LIFE

I AM

In text, letters, calls
There is
THE SAFETY of distance

DISTANCE from touch
And insecurity about BODY
No EYES no soul no body

NO body, Nobody knows
EVERY body
Everybody knows

The insecurity of FEAR
SO MANY FEARS
Fears BIG and small

In REAL LIFE

In DISTANCE lost
As expression
It sits IN THE BODY

That FEAR
Is BEAUTIFUL
Shouts YOU're ALIVE

In REAL LIFE
it lives

Life is not perfect in real life
THERE IS disappointment & LOVE
Love & DISAPPOINTMENT

In real life

THERE IS fear

LOVE BECOMES YOU

I slip back into the past
The warm bath gets cold
With time

The presence
Of breath
Of life
Of life
Of life
Restores the flow

Love becomes you
Says the heart
To no one in particular

You flower with love
Your beauty brings
Light and heat
Dancing with earth mother
Takes you to ocean waves
And stirs the flow

Love becomes you
It shines light
On your light
Love becomes you
And you become love

Love becomes you,
Passive
A comment on appearance
An observation with distance

Love becomes you
And you become love
An act of homecoming
The warmth of the eternal
A verb, a becoming
Imbibing our truth

Love becomes you
You become love

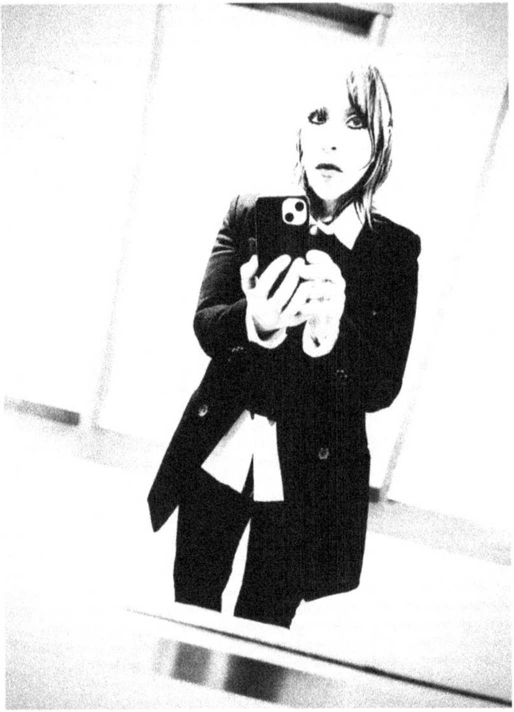

A ROSE

School girl crush
Arose in old age
Sudden desire
Flame to fire

Memory before regression
Embodiment before repression
Essence of youth, innocent truth
Sudden desire, flame to fire

Songs of love, photographs
Magazines, favourite shoes

Clothes and mirrors
Records, pins
A rose in old age, sacred sins

Flame to fire
Burning desire

Over and over
I write your name
In flowing script
Your name again

With flowers and hearts
Arose in old age
Forever apart
I whisper your name

A rose in old age
A flame from within
School girl crush
Sacred sin

EVA SAYS

Wind came back to get me
Her forsaken child
Been rockin' in the branches
Yeah, I'd been there for a while

Because the politician said
Freedom rings no longer
You can only have one child
There's a test for who is stronger

But wind is wind
Love is love
Strong is strong
And life is long
Wrong is wrong
Yeah wrong is wrong
Love is love
And life is long

The crooked banker knew the game
Back hunched over Abel's cane
Hid his money, hedged his bets
Got appointed, no regret

Bells rang loud
He wore a shroud
And threw five dollars
To the crowd

At last he owned the mushroom cloud

And then the wind
It blew away
The child grew up into a day
When winter was a memory
And water a commodity
And truth some ancient tragedy
Evaporated with the sea

And now the baby tells the tale
That honesty did once prevail
And seasons came and kindness grew
And there were trees and flowers too
People opened up their hearts
There was no final victory march
And peaceful protest part of life
And women,
They did not wear stripes
And war was done
Love it grew
Home was home
And freedom true

But wind is wind
And love is love
Strong is strong
And life is long
Wrong is wrong
Yeah, wrong is wrong
Love is love
And life is long

THE TOWER

High above the fields
High above the voices
High above the human touch
Far away from choices

Far away from human touch
Far away from noises
Far away from anything
On a bed of roses

In the tower that kept her safe
But had become a prison
In the empty room she waits
For a saviour or a vision

Without which she cannot descend
She cannot leave the tower
She does not age she does not want
With light she marks the hour

A distant dream denied by faith
Traps her in devotion
A prayer that she cannot escape
To sail across the ocean

The suitors arrive one by one
They make their case they say her name
She whispers in the prison tower
Go away go away

Freedom doesn't look like that
She counts the ways she can't accept
These suitors that would take her down
From her bed of roses

Unsuitable suitors on the ground
They tell her they will take her down
Afflicted, Conflicted, Wrongly Convicted,

Pauper, Priest, Grotesque, and Greed
None of them can see the crown
All of them would take her down

She finds a way to reconstruct
The prison and the tower
Within her heart within her mind
She holds all the power
Within her body and her soul
She shoos away the stale the mould
She cleans her house she sees a path
Was always there without a map

She sees the light beyond the door
The tower was a metaphor
For prisons we create with thought
And suitors who don't suit our plot

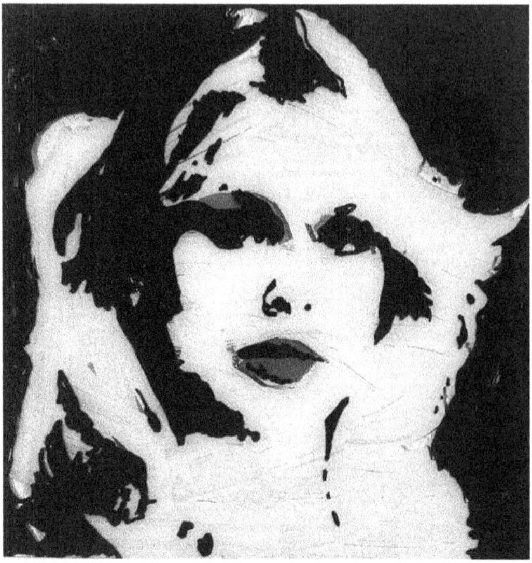

FADED

Your footprints in the snow
Melted as quickly as yesterday's plan
When you said you were leaving
And didn't go

It didn't make things better
It only made you fade
From black to drab
Like the clothes at the bottom
Of the drawer

The ones I never wear
But don't give away

LOVE POEM 7

Your kiss is a promise
Which will be broken
An attempt to stay open
Silent not spoken
Feelings expressed
Might make love or the illusion of love
Disappear
Evaporate like ether
Vanish like vapour
Disintegrate like life
Unravel like silk
Bloom and then wither
Your kiss is a promise
We know will be broken
As seasons change
And flowers fade
But today it tastes like
Honey and rose petals
Your kiss

NOT LOVE

We say it isn't love
To shield ourselves from pain
We say it's merely misting
To stay dry from rain

Standing in the shadows
Hiding from the hurt
Walking on the concrete
To save ourselves from dirt

Living in the black and white
Keeps us from the work
Waiting in the shadows
Where feelings long and lurk

Rather risk my heart in love
Than keep it safe and void
Rather cry the tears of loss
Than never truly fly
Live only on the margins
Feel only on the periphery
Breathe only in the shallow end
Of life and love and joy

LONELY HEART OF SAINT VALENTINE

She woke up alone
No different than other days
But this was a day of flowers
A day of hope
A day of cards
And chocolate kisses
A day of touch
And love songs
A day of happy couples
Holding hands
Gazing into eyes
That gazed back at theirs
She woke up alone
Jaw clenched like a fist
With nothing but memories
A silence so loud
A sadness so deep
That even her tears couldn't cry

WITH LOVE

She used to search for sadness
To cover up the pain
She found it in her body
She found it in her brain
She found it in her story
She found it in the rain
She found it in her friendships
She found it in her love
She found it in the world outside
And in the skies above
She found it every everywhere
She found it in her heart
She used to search for sadness
Now she looks for art
Now she looks for beauty
Now she looks for love
Now she's standing in the light
With love with love with love

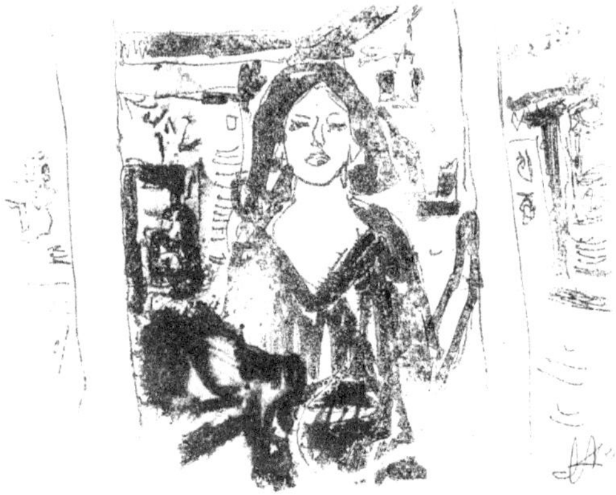

ILLUSION

Who walks with us in this illusion

Grasping mirages we believe are real

As we sidestep life for lifeless

As the wind wails and birds whisper

Springs gurgle with laughter at our folly

Flowers bloom and fall into their beds

Sand melts into the sea

Rivers run into the ocean

Breaths sigh and clocks count

Ticking and talking stories of pain and separation

Who walks with us in this illusion

Only memory, time , and thought

As vivid as reality

Who walks with us in this illusion

As love waits with open arms

And invites us to come home

ALSO OUT ON FAR WEST

SONNY VINCENT......................................Snake Pit Therapy

BRENT L. SMITH..Pipe Dreams on Pico

JOSEPH MATICK…..The Baba Books

KURT EISENLOHR..Stab the Remote

KANSAS BOWLING….....................….A Cuddly Toys Companion

KANSAS BOWLING & PARKER LOVE BOWLING…....................
             Prewritten Letters for Your Convenience

CRAIG DYER…....................Heavier Than a Death in the Family

PARKER LOVE BOWLING....................................Rhododendron,
                                               Rhododendron

JENNIFER ROBIN...............................You Only Bend Once with
                                          a Spoonful of Mercury

JOSEPH MATICK…..Cherry Wagon

RICHARD CABUT..Disorderly Magic

NORMAN DOUGLAS.................................Love and the Fear of Love

ELIZABETH ELLEN...Estranged

JEFFREY WENGROFSKY........................The Wolfboy of Rego Park

HAKON ADALSTEINSSON.......................................Our Broken Land

.A FAR WEST ANTHOLOGY..Pretty Obscure

.LILY LADY..NDA

NIKOLA PEPERA...Lay Down & Get Lost

JACK SKELLEY...Myth Lab

PETER CROWLEY...Down at Max's

STEVE KRAKOW...............................A Mind Blown Is A Mind Shown

ADDISON FULTON..Social Animals

TONY O'NEILL..Forged Prescriptions

....

farwestpress.com

+1 (541) FAR-WEST